Contents

Published: August 29, 2012

Prologue

Welcome to my first book! I am proud to say that I am finally embracing my strengths.

I have been a tax accountant for over 25 years. I am passionate about helping people claim the best legal deductions yet never shared my knowledge with anyone on a large scale. I think this stems from accountants being viewed as serious, bookworms, loners and stuffy. I can tell you I am nothing like this. I love people. I love to have fun and I also love the complexity of the tax world and helping others navigate it.

This brings me to the book, Moneybags 101: Seven Important Tax Questions for a Business Owner which I have had a desire to write for about a year. I am an expert in taxes for the home based business, real estate agent and rental property owner. I enjoy helping these clients find the best legal deductions, which saves them money.

As I work with entrepreneurial taxpayers I am consistently asked the same questions. I figured that others have the same challenge so it seemed natural to write a short book to share my knowledge. The tax laws are very complex. Moneybags 101 is designed to help you start asking the right questions and to start you on a path to larger deductions.

I hope you enjoy my first book. I am confident that you will find a tax tip that will keep some of your hard earned cash in your pocket.

There are more great tax tips at www.moneybagstaxservice.com.
I would enjoy hearing from you. Feel free to leave me a
comment or question.

Much success to you,
Carol Herzog
Moneybags Tax Service LLC
"Legal Deductions Save You Money"

Chapter 1
What business entity is best for your business?

This is an important question when people start a business. Do I need to incorporate? What are the benefits of incorporating? Can I run the business under my social security number or do I need a federal identification number?

First it would be best to understand what each business entity is. There are three types of business entities that the IRS recognizes: Sole Proprietor, Partnership and Corporation. Under the corporation category there are subcategories: Corporation (C-Corp) , Sub-chapter Corporation (S-Corp) and Limited Liability Corporation (LLC).

Each business entity has its own set of rules and tax advantages. Although this book is directed towards the sole proprietor it is important to have an understanding of each business entity. Let's look at each one separately.

Sole Proprietor

A sole proprietorship or self-employed person is the oldest and most common type of business. It exists when only one person owns and manages a business with the intent of earning a profit. A sole proprietorship is formed the moment you make your first sale or perform some other business transaction. Examples of a sole proprietorship include a bookkeeper who works from her home, a construction handyman who works on his own or a freelance consultant offering his services to local businesses. The benefits and liabilities of the sole proprietorship are different from those with other business types.

The sole proprietorship is the easiest and least expensive way to start a company. The Internal Revenue Service does not consider the sole proprietorship as a separate business entity. The owner reports income from the business on Form 1040 using Schedule C and Schedule SE. The income is taxed at their personal income tax rate plus self-employment taxes. Local and state governments may have licensing fees and reporting requirements also. This is also the easiest business to shut down – you just stop being in business.

Example 1:
Sue is a painter and artist. Sue spends most of her time creating new pieces, marketing them online and displaying her work at art shows. This is Sue's main source of income. Sue is a sole proprietor.

Partnership

A partnership is a business relationship existing between two or more people who have joined together to carry on a trade or business. Each person contributes money, property, labor or skill, and expects to share in the profits and losses of the business.

A partnership is pretty easy to set up but takes some coordinating with the other partner.
First determine which state the partnership will be in. Usually, it will be where you reside and plan to do business. Some people will advise you to set up your partnership in more tax-friendly states, but this is often more trouble than it's worth.
Second choose a name for your partnership. Make sure it is not taken by another business or confusing for your clients or customers.

Third decide the duties of each partner and how the profits will be distributed. Also decide the duties of each partner and the level of liability each partner is comfortable with.

Fourth draft the partnership agreement, including all the details described in step 3. An attorney can draft one for you. Be careful about using free online templates for your partnership agreement. They may not cover your individual circumstances.

Fifth obtain a federal tax ID number. You will need this number to open a bank account and file your tax forms.

A partnership must file an annual information return, Form 1065, to report the income, deductions, gains, losses, etc., from its operations. The partnership does not pay income tax, instead it "passes through" any profits or losses to its partners. These pass through items are reported to the partner on a Form 1065 Schedule K-1 (Partner's Share of Income, Deductions, Credits, etc.) and includes his or her share of the partnership's income or loss on their personal tax return. Partners are not employees and should not be issued a Form W-2. General partners are considered self-employed and should pay federal, state and self-employment taxes on the partnership's earnings.

There are two types of partnerships:

GENERAL PARTNERSHIPS In this standard form of partnership, all of the partners are equally responsible for the business's debts and liabilities. In addition, all partners are allowed to be involved in the management of the company. In fact, in the absence of a statement to the contrary in the partnership agreement, each partner has equal rights to control and manage the business. Therefore, unanimous consent of the partners is required for all major actions undertaken. Be advised, though, that any obligation made by one partner is legally binding on all partners, whether or not they have been informed.

LIMITED PARTNERSHIPS (LP) In a limited partnership, one or more partners are general partners, and one or more are limited partners. General partners are personally liable for the business's debts and judgments against the business; they can also be directly involved in the management. Limited partners are essentially investors (silent partners, so to speak) who do not participate in the company's management and who are also not liable beyond their investment in the business. State laws determine how involved limited partners can be in the day-to-day business of the firm without jeopardizing their limited liability. This business form is especially attractive to real estate investors, who benefit from the tax incentives available to limited partners, such as being able to write off depreciating values.

Example 2:
Joe and David decide to open an ice cream shop together called J & D Treats LP. They decide to split everything 50-50 as general partners. At the end of the year J & D Treats has made a $75,000 net profit. They file the annual Form 1065 return with the IRS and are issued K1's for their share of the profit, $37,500 each. As a general partner, Joe will report his $37,500 on his own return and pay federal, self-employment tax and state taxes. David will do the same.

Example 3:
Sharon and Dana decide to open a resale dress shop called Once Over LP. Sharon is the general partner and owns 90% of Once Over. Sharon also invests $10,000 to start the store. Dana is a limited partner and owns 10% of the company. Dana invests $200. Once Over files its first tax return sustaining a net loss of $8,000. Both women are issued a K1 for their portion of the loss. Sharon's portion of the loss is $7,200. Dana's portion of the loss is $800. Because Sharon has enough capital in the business she will be able to deduct the entire $7,200 loss. This could give Sharon a tax advantage if she has other taxable

income to net against the loss. Dana on the other hand is not allowed to claim the loss because she is a limited partner. Dana's loss is carried forward until there is income to go against it. This determination is based on the "at risk" rules and "passive activity" rules which you might want to investigate further if you are considering establishing a limited partnership.

Corporations

Corporations (C-Corp, S-Corp and LLC) offer many benefits that are not available to a sole proprietor or partnership. As a corporation it is its own separate legal entity.   The business owner creates shares of company stock, which he keeps or sells to others, which can generate cash to start the business or expand.   As a major stockholder of the company, you enter into a contract with the corporation to run the business as an employee. As an employee of the corporation you enjoy the limited liability regarding the legal obligations of the corporation.   Any financial obligations required by the company fall solely on the company and do not transfer to any employee. As an employee your financial assets remain protected from any legal action against the company. Corporations have full discretion over the amount of profits they can distribute or retain. Corporations are presumed to be for-profit entities, and as such they can have an unlimited number of years with losses. Corporations must have at least one shareholder.

To incorporate your business, you will need to write up your Articles of Incorporation, By-Laws, file various documents with your state government, obtain an Employer Identification Number (EIN) from the IRS, and once approved, submit these documents to your bank to set up a business bank account. State governments charge filing fees for processing your incorporation documents. You might also need to file a Doing

Business As form with your county government to register your business name, and this requires a filing fee and newspaper costs for announcing your business name to the public. These fees can quickly add up, so have solid reasons for incorporating, and understand how your form of organization will achieve your business, legal, and tax needs.

IRS Form 1120, U.S. Corporation Income Tax Return, is used to report the income, gains, losses, deductions, credits, and to figure the income tax liability of a corporation.

S-Corporations

Like a C corporation, S corporations are merely corporations that elect to pass corporate income, losses, deductions, and credit through to their shareholders for federal tax purposes. The S status combines the legal environment of C corporations with U.S. federal income taxation similar to that of partnerships. As with partnerships, the income, deductions, and tax credits of an S corporation flow through to shareholders annually, regardless of whether distributions of income were made. Thus, income is taxed at the shareholder level and not at the corporate level. Also, certain corporate penalty taxes (e.g., accumulated earnings tax, personal holding company tax) and the alternative minimum tax do not apply to an S corporation.

An S corporation is not eligible for a dividend received deduction like the C-Corp is. Nor is it subject to the 10 percent of taxable income limitation applicable to charitable contribution deductions.

S corporation shareholders are employees of the corporation and are paid a fair wage for their service. Any distribution after "fair wages" has been paid can be a distribution of profit, return of capital or repayment of loan and will be treated as such for taxes.

IRS Form 1120S, U.S. Corporation Income Tax Return, is used to report the income, gains, losses, deductions, credits. These items are then passed through to the shareholder using the reporting form 1120S K-1.

Qualification for S corporation status

In order to make an election to be treated as an S corporation, the following requirements must be met:

- Must be an eligible entity (a domestic corporation, or a limited liability company which has elected to be taxed as a corporation).
- Must have only one class of stock.
- Must not have more than 100 shareholders.
  - Spouses are automatically treated as a single shareholder.
- Shareholders must be U.S. citizens or residents, and must be natural persons
- Profits and losses must be allocated to shareholders proportionately to each one's interest in the business.

In order to become an S corporation, the corporation must submit Form 2553 Election by a Small Business Corporation signed by all the shareholders in a timely manner. Relief for a late election may be available if the corporation can show that the failure to file on time was due to reasonable cause.

When to Make the Election

Complete and file Form 2553:

No more than two months and 15 days after the beginning of the tax year the election is to take effect, or
At any time during the tax year preceding the tax year it is to take effect.

Example 4:
No prior tax year.   A calendar year small business corporation begins its first tax year on January 7. The two month period ends March 6 and 15 days after that is March 21. To be an S corporation beginning with its first tax year, the corporation must file IRS Form 2553 during the period that begins January 7 and ends March 21. Because the corporation had no prior tax year, an election made before January 7 will not be valid.

Example 5:
Prior tax year.   A calendar year small business corporation has been filing Form 1120 as a C corporation but wishes to make an S election for its next tax year beginning January 1. The two month period ends February 28 (29 in leap years) and 15 days after that is March 15. To be an S corporation beginning with its next tax year, the corporation must file Form 2553 during the period that begins the first day (January 1) of its last year as a C corporation and ends March 15th of the year it wishes to be an S corporation. Because the corporation had a prior tax year, it can make the election at any time during that prior tax year.

The service center will notify the corporation if its election is accepted and when it will take effect. The corporation will also be notified if its election is not accepted. The corporation should generally receive a determination on its election within 60 days after it has filed Form 2553.

Limited Liability Corporation

A Limited Liability Company (LLC) is a business structure allowed by state statute. LLCs are popular because, similar to a corporation, owners have limited personal liability for the debts and actions of the LLC. Other features of LLCs are more like a partnership, providing management flexibility and the benefit of pass-through taxation.

Owners of an LLC are called members. Since most states do not restrict ownership, members may include individuals, corporations, other LLCs and foreign entities. There is no maximum number of members. Most states also permit "single member" LLCs, those having only one owner.

The federal government does not recognize an LLC as a classification for federal tax purposes. When you form a limited liability company (LLC), it is automatically assigned a "default" tax status unless you choose otherwise. One-member LLCs are generally taxed as sole proprietorships, and those with multiple members are taxed as partnerships.

It's important, though, to have the best-available tax classification for your LLC in order to maximize your tax savings. After learning more about each business entity, you may decide that it's advantageous for your LLC to change its tax status. You can accomplish this by filing Internal Revenue Service Form 8832.

By filing Form 8832 with the IRS, you can choose a tax status for your entity besides the default status. You have the option to have your LLC be taxed as a sole proprietorship, partnership, C Corporation or S Corporation. In some cases, by changing its tax status, a company can save thousands of dollars in taxes as well as increase your liability protection.

When to make the election

The election to be taxed as the new entity will be in effect on the date the LLC enters on line 8 of Form 8832. This election cannot be 75 days before the filing date nor can it be more than 12 months passed the filing date. The IRS does provide relief for a late election (more than 75 days before the filing of the Form 8832) if the late filing is due to a reasonable cause.

Which entity do I chose?

When I am talking with a client about setting up their business I always ask this important question. Does your service or product have a high probability for liability?

    a. **Example 6:** You manufacture a small child's toy. What is the possibility of a child swallowing the toy? What is the possibility of the toy having edges that could hurt the child?
        i. Your business entity might need the additional liability protection that the C-Corp or S-Corp could provide.
    b. **Example 7:** You are a one person web designer team. What are the possibilities of someone physically getting hurt?
        i. Your business entity probably does not hold a high probability of someone getting hurt so you might chose a sole proprietor business entity and purchase a good error and omission insurance policy.
    c. **Example 8:** You and your best friend make cookies for a living. The business has grown to include 5 employees. What are the possibilities that one of your employees will burn themselves and it is determined that the oven malfunctioned due to lack of maintenance.

i. If you have a partnership under this scenario both partners would be legally responsible. If your business entity was an LLC and taxed as an S-Corp your liability would be limited.

Choosing the correct business entity is an important decision. Take the time to investigate by searching on the internet, asking other business owner what they chose and why, and talking to a lawyer or tax professional.

Please visit www.moneybagstaxservice.com to learn more about the tax laws.

Resources

Sole Proprietor

 Sole Proprietorship - type, disadvantages, cost, Advantages of sole proprietorship http://www.referenceforbusiness.com/small/Sm-Z/Sole-Proprietorship.html#ixzz2294aXy77
http://www.ehow.com/info_7900043_sole-proprietorship.html
http://www.poznaklaw.com/Doing-Business-as-a-Sole-Proprietor.shtml

Partnership

http://en.wikipedia.org/wiki/Partnership
http://www.ehow.com/how_2307858_set-up-partnership.html
http://www.irs.gov/businesses/small/article/0,,id=98214,00.html
http://www.inc.com/articles/1999/10/14602_html
http://www.referenceforbusiness.com/small/Op-Qu/Partnership.html

S-Corporation

http://en.wikipedia.org/wiki/S_corporation
http://www.irs.gov/businesses/small/article/0,,id=98263,00.html

Limited Liability Corporation

https://www.incorporate.com/form8832.html
http://www.irs.gov/businesses/small/article/0,,id=98277,00.html

Chapter 2
Am I conducting a business or a hobby?

The Internal Revenue Service asks you to follow appropriate guidelines when determining whether an activity is a business or a hobby. An activity qualifies as a business if it is carried on with the reasonable expectation of earning a profit. A hobby is an activity not engaged in for profit. Incorrect deduction of hobby expenses account for a portion of the overstated adjustments, deductions, exemptions and credits that add up to $30 billion per year in unpaid taxes, according to IRS estimates.

In general, taxpayers may deduct ordinary and necessary expenses for conducting a business. An ordinary expense is an expense that is common and accepted in the taxpayer's business. A necessary expense is one that is appropriate for the business. In order to make this determination, taxpayers should consider the following factors:

- ❖ **Does the time and effort put into the activity indicate an intention to make a profit?**
  - o Are you putting in consistent effort every day?
  - o Are you promoting your business when you are out in public?
    - ▪ Are you handing out business cards?
    - ▪ Do you share with others what you do?
  - o Do you belong to a professional organization within your industry?
  - o Does the business have its own checking account and credit cards?
- ❖ **Does the taxpayer depend on income from the activity?**
  - o Do you use the income to pay bills or save for retirement?

- o If you closed the business would it have a significant impact on your finances?
- ❖ **If there are losses, are they due to circumstances beyond the taxpayer's control or did they occur in the start-up phase of the business?**
  - o Having a loss in the start-up phase of your business can be considered normal. When you start a business, money is spent on furniture, brochures, licenses etc. Plus the income in this phase can be inconsistent.
  - o Do you have a loss because of a theft or natural disaster?
- ❖ **Has the taxpayer changed methods of operation to improve profitability?**
  - o Are you trying new business activities to see what creates profit or are you sticking with the same activities that do not generate income?
- ❖ **Does the taxpayer or his/her advisors have the knowledge needed to carry on the activity as a successful business?**
  - o Do you have knowledge of this business? Are you a nurse wanting to open up a restaurant or are you a nurse wanting to open up a nursing home?
- ❖ **Has the taxpayer made a profit in similar activities in the past?**
  - o Have you made money doing a similar activity? Did the nurse work in a hospital or doctor's office before wanting to open up a nursing home? Did the nurse's family own a successful restaurants and she grew up working side by side with her parents in this business?
- ❖ **Does the activity make a profit in some years?**
  - o The IRS presumes that an activity is carried on for profit if it makes a profit during at least three

of the last five tax years, including the current year. Note: If you have documented your expenses properly and have conducted yourself as a business it would be difficult for the IRS to disallow the business loss.
- ❖ **Can the taxpayer expect to make a profit in the future from the appreciation of assets used in the activity?**
  - ○ Let's say that your business purchased a large piece of equipment and you have chosen to expense it in a short period of time. This business decision might generate a loss for tax purposes. When this piece of equipment is fully expensed would your business generate a profit?

Example 9:
Jane enjoys scrap booking and even started a scrap booking club. A couple times of year Jane rents a booth at the local mall to sell some of her ideas and items.   Jane has a business card, pays for everything out of her personal account and spends about 5 hours per week on scrap booking.   Jane is operating this activity as a hobby.

Example 10:
The same Jane as example 9 but this time Jane decides that she needs to bring in some additional money for the family.   Jane sets up a separate checking and credit card account. She attends local chamber events, rents booth space every quarter, tells people that she meets what she does, has invested in inventory and pays herself out of the profits. Jane is now conducting this activity as a business.

Keep in mind, if an activity is not for profit (hobby), losses from that activity may not be used to offset other income.

Please visit www.moneybagstaxservice.com to learn more about legal tax deductions for your business.

Resources:

http://www.irs.gov/newsroom/article/0,,id=169490,00.html

Chapter 3
What are my self-employed tax obligations?

As a self-employed individual, generally you are required to file an annual return and pay estimated tax quarterly.

Self-employed individuals generally must pay self-employment tax (SE tax) as well as income tax. SE tax is a Social Security and Medicare tax primarily for individuals who work for themselves. It is similar to the Social Security and Medicare taxes withheld from the pay of most wage earners. In general, anytime the wording "self-employment tax" is used; it only refers to Social Security and Medicare taxes and not any other tax (like income tax).

Before you can determine if you are subject to self-employment tax and income tax, you must figure your net profit or net loss from your business. You do this by subtracting your business expenses from your business income. If your expenses are less than your income, the difference is net profit and becomes part of your income on page 1 of Form 1040. If your expenses are more than your income, the difference is a net loss. You usually can deduct your loss from gross income on page 1 of Form 1040. But in some situations your loss is limited.

You should file an income tax return and pay SE tax if your net earnings are $400 or more. If your net earnings from self-employment were less than $400, you should still file an income tax return but you would not owe SE tax.

How Do I Make My Quarterly Payments?

Estimated tax is the method used to pay Social Security and Medicare taxes and income tax, because you do not have an employer withholding these taxes for you. Form 1040-ES, Estimated Tax for Individuals, is used to figure these taxes. Use the worksheet found in Form 1040-ES, Estimated Tax for Individuals to find out if you are required to file quarterly estimated tax.

Form 1040-ES also contains blank vouchers you can use when you mail your estimated tax payments or you may make your payments using the Electronic Federal Tax Payment System (EFTPS). If this is your first year being self-employed, you will need to estimate the amount of income you expect to earn for the year. If you estimated your earnings too high, simply complete another Form 1040-ES worksheet to refigure your estimated tax for the next quarter. If you estimated your earnings too low, again complete another Form 1040-ES worksheet to recalculate your estimated taxes for the next quarter.

How Do I File My Annual Return?

To file your yearly tax return, you will need to use Schedule C or Schedule C - EZ to report your income or loss from a business you operated or a profession you practiced as a sole proprietor.

Small businesses and statutory employees with expenses of $5,000 or less may be able to file Schedule C-EZ instead of the long Schedule C form. In order to report your Social Security and Medicare taxes, you must file Schedule SE (Form 1040), Self-Employment Tax. Use the income or loss calculated on Schedule C or Schedule C-EZ to calculate the amount of Social Security and Medicare taxes you should have paid during the year.

The Instructions for Schedule C and Schedule SE may be helpful in filing out the form. You can also find forms and instructions at www.irs.gov.

Example 11
Joshua reviews his income and expenses each quarter as a self-employed writer. He has determined that from January to March he earned $10,000 and his expenses were $2,000. This gave him a taxable profit for the first quarter of $8,000. He has figured that his federal tax rate is 10% and self-employment tax is 15.3% for a total of 25.3%. He multiplies his profit of $8,000 by 25.3% to calculate his tax liability of $2,024. Joshua then sends a check for $2,024 to the United States Treasury using form 1040-ES. Joshua also remembers to put in the memo section of the check: the year, the quarter, the form number and the last 4 digits of his social security number (Year 2012, 1st qtr, Form 1040ES, SS #1234). By adding this notation the IRS knows exactly where Joshua wants the money applied. Joshua then applies the same process to his state taxes.

Please visit www.moneybagstaxservice.com to learn more about legal tax deductions for Schedule C.

Resources:

http://www.irs.gov/businesses/small/selfemployed/index.html

Chapter 4
How do I record my income and expenses correctly?

Now that you have started your business and decided what kind of business entity is best for you the next step is to document your income and expenses.

Per the IRS, business income is income received from the sale of products or services. For example, fees received by a professional person are considered business income. Rents received by a person in the real estate business are business income. Payments received in the form of property or services must be included in income at their fair market value.

Per the IRS, for the expense to be deductible it must be both ordinary and necessary. An ordinary expense is one that is common and accepted in your trade or business. A necessary expense is one that is helpful and appropriate for your trade or business. An expense does not have to be indispensable to be considered necessary.

Let me stress how important proper documentation is. The IRS audits more self-employed business owners than any other taxpayer. Why? As a business owner you are allowed to write off expenses that an employee cannot. Also, if your lifestyle is bigger than your income this might trigger an audit.

With proper documentation and a few simple rules you can be on your way to receiving the best legal tax deductions.

Business items should be kept separate from your personal items. If you intermingle personal and business the IRS could determine that your business is actually a hobby.

One of the very first things to do is to set up a designated checking account. Everything that happens in your business affects the check-book, it is where **all income and expenses are recorded.** Business checking accounts can have bank service fees so try asking your local bank for a free personal checking account. The important thing is that this account is only used for business. The IRS will not like it if you write a check to the grocery store out of your business account. Also you should have a separate credit card for your business. This is a card that only business items are charged on.

The first expenses that you might incur are **start-up costs**. Per the IRS start-up cost are amounts paid or incurred for: **(a)** creating an active trade or business; or **(b)** investigating the creation or acquisition of an active trade or business

A qualified start-up cost is amortizable (expensed usually over a 60 month period) if it meets both of the following tests.

- It is a cost you could deduct if you paid or incurred it to operate an existing active trade or business.
- It is a cost you pay or incur before the day your active trade or business begins.

Start-up costs include amounts paid for the following:

- An analysis or survey of potential markets, products, labor supply, transportation facilities, etc.
- Advertisements for the opening of the business.

- Salaries and wages for employees who are being trained and their instructors.
- Travel and other necessary costs for securing prospective distributors, suppliers, or customers.
- Salaries and fees for executives and consultants, or for similar professional services.

The next expenses that you incur will be the **day to day business expenses**. These expenses include advertising, insurance, interest, accounting fees, car expense, office expense, rental of equipment or office space, office supplies, travel expenses, meal expenses, utilities and other cost to operate your business. Documentation is key in making these deductions audit proof. Please keep your receipts with a note as to how and when it was paid. Also your meal receipts should be noted with whom you meet and what your business activity was. <u>Notation on the receipt:</u> You meet John Smith to discuss the prospect of him becoming your client. The meal receipt should also have the restaurant's name and date on it.

Lastly, there are **capital expenses.** Capital expenses are payments by a business for fixed assets, like buildings and equipment. Capital expenses are not used for ordinary day-to-day operating expenses of a business, like rent, utilities, and insurance. Another way to consider capital expenses is that they are used to buy assets that have a useful life of more than one year.

For example, if you buy office supplies for your business, that purchase is a day to day or operating expense, because office supplies don't typically last more than one year (although you may have those boxes of staples lying around for a long time). On the other hand, if you buy office furniture, it is expected that it will last longer than a year, so you are buying a fixed asset, and that purchase is considered a capital expense.

Depreciation is used to take a deduction for Capital Expenses allowing a taxpayer to recover the cost or other basis of certain property over its useful life. It is an annual allowance (expense) for the wear and tear, deterioration, or obsolescence of the property. Office furniture is expensed over its useful life of seven years while computers are expensed over five years.

Do you have a question about an expense you might want to deduct. Please visit www.moneybagstaxservice.com and leave me a comment or question. I will do my best to answer it.

Resources

http://www.irs.gov/businesses/small/article/0,,id=109807,00.html
http://www.irs.gov/taxtopics/tc407.html
http://biztaxlaw.about.com/od/glossaryc/a/capitalexpense.htm
http://www.irs.gov/publications/p535/ch08.html

Chapter 5
Do I choose actual or standard mileage for my automobile expense?

If you own your own business, you likely have vehicle expenses. A major potential deduction as a business expense may be the use of your vehicle. To claim this deduction is it important to keep proper written records. These records include the date, beginning odometer reading, ending odometer reading, total miles and your business activity. When you complete your return it will be necessary to have: total miles the car was driven for the year, total business miles and total commuting miles to calculate your deduction.

The IRS defines a "car" as any four-wheeled vehicle (including a truck or van), under 6,000 pounds, that is made primarily for use on public streets. An ambulance, hearse or bus do not qualify under these rules.t qualify. There are special rules for vehicle that weigh more than 6,000 pounds. Please visit Publication 463 *Travel, Entertainment, Gifts and Car* expense to learn more.

There are two acceptable methods by which the IRS allows one to deduct vehicle expenses - the *standard mileage rate* or the *actual expenses*. If you qualify to use both methods you may want to figure your deduction both ways to see which gives you a larger deduction.

Standard Mileage Rate:

The standard mileage rate is a determined amount by the IRS to operate your car. For year 2012 that rate is $0.555 per mile.

This rate includes the expenses for gas, oil changes, repairs, car washes, registration fees, licenses and insurance. In addition to the mileage rate you can claim the business percent for the loan interest and personal property tax as well as any business-related parking fees and tolls.

If you choose to deduct the standard mileage rate for a car you own, you must do so in the first year the car is available for use in your business. By doing this you have the option of claiming the standard mileage rate or actual expenses in later years.

For a leased vehicle, if you use the standard mileage rate you must continue to use this method over the life of the lease.

To use the standard mileage rate, you must own or lease the car and:

- You must not operate five or more cars at the same time, as in a fleet operation. Beginning in 2011, you can elect to use the standard mileage rate if you used less than five cars for hire (such as a taxi).
- You must not have claimed a depreciation deduction using the Modified Accelerated Cost Recovery System (MACRS) on the car in an earlier year, including any additional first-year depreciation or "bonus depreciation" or any method other than straight-line for its estimated useful life
- You must not have claimed a Section 179 deduction on the car; and you must not have claimed actual expenses after 1997 for a car you leased, and
- You cannot use the standard mileage rate if you are a rural mail carrier who received a "qualified reimbursement"

Example 12

Joe owns a local bakery. Joe drives to the bakery to open the shop. He then drives to the supply store to pick up more flour and to the bank to drop off a deposit. At the end of the day Joe drives home.   Joe's drive to the bakery and home are commuting miles and are not business deductions. When Joe drove to the supply store and bank he should write down his beginning odometer reading, ending odometer reading, how many miles and business activity (picking up baking supplies and deposit at the bank). The miles to the supply store and bank are deductible business miles.

Example 13
Marcia, a salesperson, owns three cars and two vans that she alternates using for calling on her customers. She can use the standard mileage rate for the business mileage of the three cars and the two vans because she does not use them at the same time.

Please refer to Publication 463, *Travel, Entertainment, Gift and Car Expenses*, for the current standard mileage rate. Another great resource is www.moneybagstaxservice.com.

Actual expense:

To use the actual expense method, you must determine what it actually costs to operate the car. This includes gas, oil, repairs, tires, car washes, road side assistance, insurance, registration fees, licenses, and depreciation (or lease payments). Next, you would figure the business portion based on how many personal miles and business miles that were driven.

Parking fees and tolls attributable to business use are separately deductible, just as they are in the standard mileage rate method.

If you decide to take actual expense it will be necessary to do further research on depreciation rules and limitations.

Example 14

Maureen owns a car and four vans that are used in her housecleaning business. Her employees use the vans, and she uses the car to travel to various customers. Maureen cannot use the standard mileage rate for the car or the vans. This is because all five vehicles are used in Maureen's business at the same time. She must use actual expenses for all vehicles. Also the vans would be 100% business because they stay at the business location overnight.

Example 15
Standard mileage vs. Actual

John has a 4 year old car and has used the standard mileage rates since the first year. This year he had a substantial car repair bills so he decided to calculate both methods to see what would give him the larger deduction. John drove a total of 17,362 miles with 10,362 of them being for business.

Under the IRS standard miles rate, for year 2012, John's deduction would be $5,751 (10,362 X $0.555 per mile).

Under the actual method, John spent $3,424 for gas, $600 for insurance, $1,500 for the repair, $50 for registration, $135 for road side assistance and $50 for car washes. John also is allowed a depreciation deduction of $1775. This is a total cost of $7,534. John did not drive his car 100% for business so the business percentage will be based on the miles driven. Divide the business miles by the total miles (10,362/17,362) for a business percent of 59.7%. Multiply the total cost $7,534 by 59.7% for a deduction of $4,498.

If John uses the standard deduction his business expense would be $5,751. If he uses the actual expense his business expense would be $4,498.

Under this example it would be in John's best interest to use the standard miles even though he had to pay a large amount for the repair.

Resources

http://voices.yahoo.com/the-irs-standard-mileage-rate-vs-actual-car-expenses-7937390.html?cat=3
http://www.irs.gov/publications/p463/ch04.html#en_US_2011_publink100033930

Chapter 6
I work from Home. Can I Claim a Deduction?

Whether you are self-employed or an employee, if you use a portion of your home for business, you may be able to take a home office deduction. Here are <u>five</u> things the IRS wants you to know about the Home Office deduction

First: Generally, in order to claim a business deduction for your home, you must use part of your home <u>exclusively and regularly,</u> as your principal place of business, or as a place to meet or deal with patients, clients or customers in the normal course of your business, or in any connection with your trade or business where the business portion of your home is a separate structure not attached to your home.

As your Principal Place of Business

You can have more than one business location, including your home, for a single trade or business. To qualify to deduct the expenses for the business use of your home under the principal place of business test, your home must be your principal place of business for that trade or business. To determine whether your home is your principal place of business, you must consider:

- The relative importance of the activities performed at each place where you conduct business, and
- The amount of time spent at each place where you conduct business.

Your home office will qualify as your principal place of business if you meet the following requirements.

- You use it exclusively and regularly for administrative or management activities of your trade or business. There are many activities that are administrative or managerial in nature. The following are a few examples:
    Billing customers, clients, or patients.
    Keeping books and records.
    Ordering supplies.
    Setting up appointments.
    Forwarding orders or writing reports.

- You have no other fixed location where you conduct substantial administrative or management activities of your trade or business.

Example 16

Paul is a self-employed anesthesiologist. He spends the majority of his time administering anesthesia and postoperative care in three local hospitals. One of the hospitals provides him with a small shared office where he could conduct administrative or management activities.

Paul very rarely uses the office the hospital provides. He uses a room in his home that he has converted to an office. He uses this room exclusively and regularly to conduct all the following activities.

Contacting patients, surgeons, and hospitals regarding scheduling.
Preparing for treatments and presentations.
Maintaining billing records and patient logs.
Satisfying continuing medical education requirements.
Reading medical journals and books.

Paul's home office qualifies as his principal place of business for deducting expenses for its use. He conducts administrative or management activities for his business as an anesthesiologist there and he has no other fixed location where he conducts substantial administrative or management activities for this business. His choice to use his home office instead of the one provided by the hospital does not disqualify his home office from being his principal place of business. His performance of substantial non-administrative or non-management activities at fixed locations outside his home also does not disqualify his home office from being his principal place of business. He meets all the qualifications, including principal place of business, so he can deduct expenses (to the extent of the deduction limit, explained later) for the business use of his home.

OR

As a place to meet or deal with patients, clients or customers in the normal course of your business,

If you meet or deal with patients, clients, or customers in your home in the normal course of your business, even though you also carry on business at another location, you can deduct your expenses for the part of your home used exclusively and regularly for business if you meet both the following tests.

- You physically meet with patients, clients, or customers on your premises.
- Their use of your home is substantial and integral to the conduct of your business.

Doctors, dentists, attorneys, and other professionals who maintain offices in their homes generally will meet this requirement.

Using your home for occasional meetings and telephone calls will not qualify you to deduct expenses for the business use of your home.

The part of your home you use exclusively and regularly to meet patients, clients, or customers does not have to be your principal place of business.

Example 17
June Quill, a self-employed attorney, works 3 days a week in her city office. She works 2 days a week in her home office used only for business. She regularly meets clients there. Her home office qualifies for a business deduction because she meets clients there in the normal course of her business.

OR

In any connection with your trade or business where the business portion of your home is a separate structure not attached to your home.

You can deduct expenses for a separate free-standing structure, such as a studio, workshop, garage, or barn, if you use it exclusively and regularly for your business. The structure does not have to be your principal place of business or a place where you meet patients, clients, or customers.

Example 18
John Berry operates a floral shop in town. He grows the plants for his shop in a greenhouse behind his home. He uses the greenhouse exclusively and regularly in his business, so he can deduct the expenses for its use.

Second: Generally, the amount you can deduct depends on the percentage of your home used for business. Your deduction for certain expenses will be limited if your gross income from your business is less than your total business expenses.

Business Percentage
To find the business percentage, compare the part of your home that you use for business to the whole house. You can use any reasonable method to determine the business percentage. The following are two commonly used methods for figuring the percentage.
Divide the area (length multiplied by the width) used for business by the total area of your home.
If the rooms in your home are all about the same size, you can divide the number of rooms used for business by the total number of rooms in your home.
Use the resulting percentage to figure the business part of the expenses for operating your entire home.

Example 19
Your office is 120 square feet (12 feet × 10 feet).
Your home is 1,200 square feet.
Your office is 10% (120 ÷ 1,200) of the total area of your home.
Your business percentage is 10%.

Deduction Limit
If you're gross income from the business use of your home equals or exceeds your total business expenses (including depreciation), you can deduct all your business expenses related to the use of your home.

If your gross income from the business use of your home is less than your total business expenses, your deduction for certain expenses for the business use of your home is limited. The IRS does not allow your business loss to be larger due to insurance, repairs or utilities expense. These un-allowed expenses are carried forward to next year, subject to the same limitation.

Third: There are special rules for qualified daycare providers and for persons storing business inventory or product samples, you are required to use the property regularly but not exclusively.

Daycare Facility- If you use space in your home on a regular basis for providing daycare, you may be able to deduct the business expenses for that part of your home even if you use the same space for nonbusiness purposes. To qualify for this exception to the exclusive use rule, you must meet <u>both</u> of the following requirements.
1. You must be in the trade or business of providing daycare for children, persons age 65 or older, or persons who are physically or mentally unable to care for themselves.
2. You must have applied for, been granted, or be exempt from having, a license, certification, registration, or approval as a daycare center or as a family or group daycare home under state law. You do not meet this requirement if your application was rejected or your license or other authorization was revoked.

If the use of part of your home as a daycare facility is regular, but not exclusive, you must figure the percentage of time that part of your home is used for daycare. To find the percentage of time you actually use your home for business, compare the total time used for business to the total time that part of your home can be used for all purposes. A room that is available for use throughout each business day and that you regularly use in your business is considered to be used for daycare throughout each business day. You do not have to keep records to show the specific hours the area was used for business. You can use the area occasionally for personal reasons. However, a room you use only occasionally for business does not qualify for the deduction.

Storage of inventory or product samples. If you use part of your home for storage of inventory or product samples, you can deduct expenses for the business use of your home without meeting the exclusive use test. However, you must meet all the following tests.

- You sell products at wholesale or retail as your trade or business.
- You keep the inventory or product samples in your home for use in your trade or business.
- Your home is the only fixed location of your trade or business.
- You use the storage space on a regular basis.
- The space you use is a separately identifiable space suitable for storage.

Example 20
Your home is the only fixed location of your business of selling mechanics' tools at retail. You regularly use half of your basement for storage of inventory and product samples. You sometimes use the area for personal purposes. The expenses for the storage space are deductible even though you do not use this part of your basement exclusively for business.

Fourth: If you are self-employed, use Form 8829, Expenses for Business Use of Your Home to figure your home office deduction and report those deductions on Form 1040- Schedule C, Profit or Loss from Business.

Fifth: If you are an employee, additional rules and limitation apply for claiming the home office deduction. For example, the regular and exclusive business use must be for the convenience of your employer.

Example 21

Kathleen is employed as a teacher. She is required to teach and meet with students at the school and to grade papers and tests. The school provides her with a small office where she can work on her lesson plans, grade papers and tests, and meet with parents and students. The school does not require her to work at home.

Kathleen prefers to use the office she has set up in her home and does not use the one provided by the school. She uses this home office exclusively and regularly for the administrative duties of her teaching job.

Kathleen must meet the convenience-of-the-employer test, even if her home qualifies as her principal place of business for deducting expenses for its use. Her employer provides her with an office and does not require her to work at home, so she does not meet the convenience- of-the-employer test and cannot claim a deduction for the business use of her home.

The home office deduction is one of the most misunderstood. If I can help you understand this deduction better please ask me a question at www.moneybagstaxservice.com.

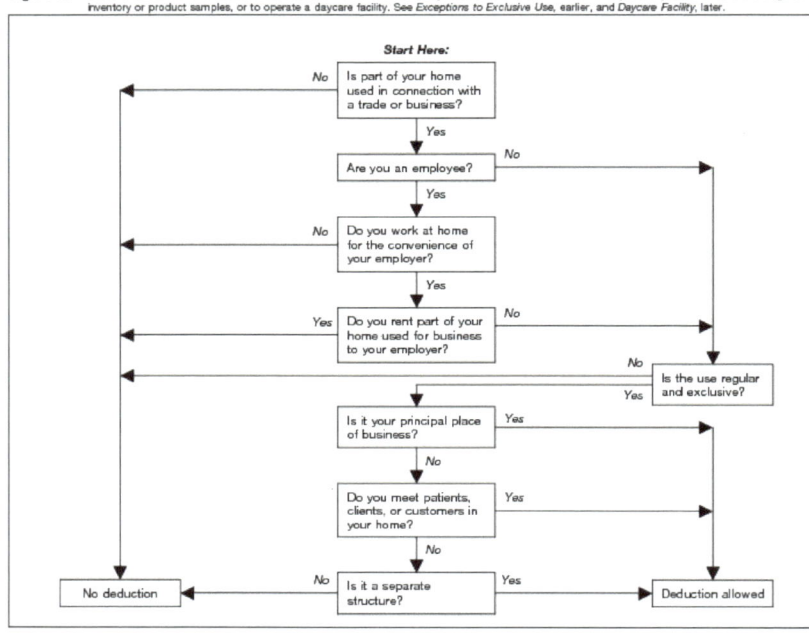

Figure A. **Can You Deduct Business Use of the Home Expenses?** Do not use this chart if you use your home for the storage of inventory or product samples, or to operate a daycare facility. See *Exceptions to Exclusive Use*, earlier, and *Daycare Facility*, later.

Resources:

http://www.irs.gov/newsroom/article/0%2C%2Cid=108138%2C00.html
http://www.irs.gov/publications/p587/ar02.html#en_US_2011_publink1000226292

Chapter 7
Why is it important to choose the right tax preparer to complete your return?

If you are like most people tax time is something you do not look forward to. Having someone on your side can help make this time of year less stressful.

Congress likes to change the tax laws almost every year so it is important to have someone on your financial team that will work with you.

The tax preparer should:
Be friendly.
Make you feel comfortable.
Ask you questions, personally, not just have you fill out a tax organizer.
Be available by person or phone all year around.
Complete your return within three weeks of giving them your information.
Be willing to do tax research on your behalf.
Educates you and helps you find more legal tax deductions.
Be able to explain the tax laws in an easy to understand method.

The IRS has recently changed the requirements for all tax preparers. You should hire someone who has the proper tax credentials as a:
1) Registered Tax Return Preparers have passed an IRS test establishing minimal competency. The test covers only individual income tax returns (Form 1040). They must adhere to ethical standards. They must also complete 15 hours of

continuing education each year. RTRPs have limited practice rights before the IRS, which means they can represent clients in only certain circumstances.

2) <u>Enrolled Agents</u> have passed a three-part, comprehensive IRS exam covering individual and business returns. They must adhere to ethical standards and complete 72 hours of continuing education courses every three years. EAs have unlimited practice rights before the IRS, which means they can represent clients for any tax matter. Their education is specifically in tax laws and tax preparation.

3) A <u>Certified Public Accountant (CPA)</u> is educated in accounting, budgeting, auditing and financial records. This education makes it a natural fit to prepare taxes. CPAs have unlimited practice rights before the IRS. The person who is a CPA has professional education that they must complete every year to keep their CPA status.

4) <u>Attorneys</u> can also prepare a tax return. This is commonly done when they are handling a trust or an estate return. Attorneys have unlimited practice rights before the IRS.

I would recommend interviewing a tax preparer before hiring them. It would be best to do this prior to tax season so they can look over your return and give you a price estimate. This also gives you time to get to know them which are an important part of adding someone to your financial support team.

Conclusion

This e-book is just a small sampling of what tax advantages are available as an entrepreneurial. We discussed which business entity would be best and whether you are conducting yourselves in a business manner or treating it like a hobby. You had an opportunity to review the taxes that you might owe and how to record your income and expenses correctly. The correct reporting of your automobile records is one item the IRS constantly holds taxpayers accountable for. It is also one that is most over looked by taxpayers. Working from home has a lot of tax and personal advantages. I just read that 1 in 5 people work from home now, thanks to the internet. Lastly, how important it is to have a team of quality and qualified people on your success team. That includes a great tax accountant.

I would like to personally thank you for purchasing my book. My core desire it that you found some value in it.

Please visit my blog at www.moneybagstaxservice.com. Leave me a comment or question if you like.

Wishing you abundance in all areas of your life,
Carol Herzog
Enrolled Agent
August 29, 2012

About the Author

Hi, I am Carol Herzog and owner of Moneybags Tax Service LLC. I live in the heart of the United States, in the Show Me State, Missouri. My husband and I have been married for 27 years and have 4 children and 4 grandchildren. We love to travel. As a family we have been to Hawaii, Alaska, Costa Rico, Cancun and all over the United States. We just finished a 14 day trip to Italy. Next year we look forward to traveling to Germany.

What I Do

I have a passion to help people save money through educating them about legal tax deductions. I am an Enrolled Agent before the IRS. This means I have the same status in front of the IRS as a CPA or tax lawyer. The main difference is my education is specifically in individual income taxes.

My tax specialty is self-employed business: Real Estate agents, Home Based Businesses, Direct Sales, Multi-Level marketing, etc. I can also prepare returns in all 50 states.

Why I Do It

I prepare taxes because I love how the numbers come together. The simplicity of two plus two equals four makes sense to me. I also enjoy helping others and educating them on something that can be very confusing at times.

How to Connect With Me

I love to stay connected with the people who enjoy my e-book and blog. If you would like more information on legal tax deductions please visit: Moneybags Tax Service LLC

Also, feel free to connect on and if you're active on these networks.

Disclaimer

www.ingramcontent.com/pod-product-compliance
Lightning Source LLC
Chambersburg PA
CBHW041112180526
45172CB00001B/219